Costa Rica

Tracey West

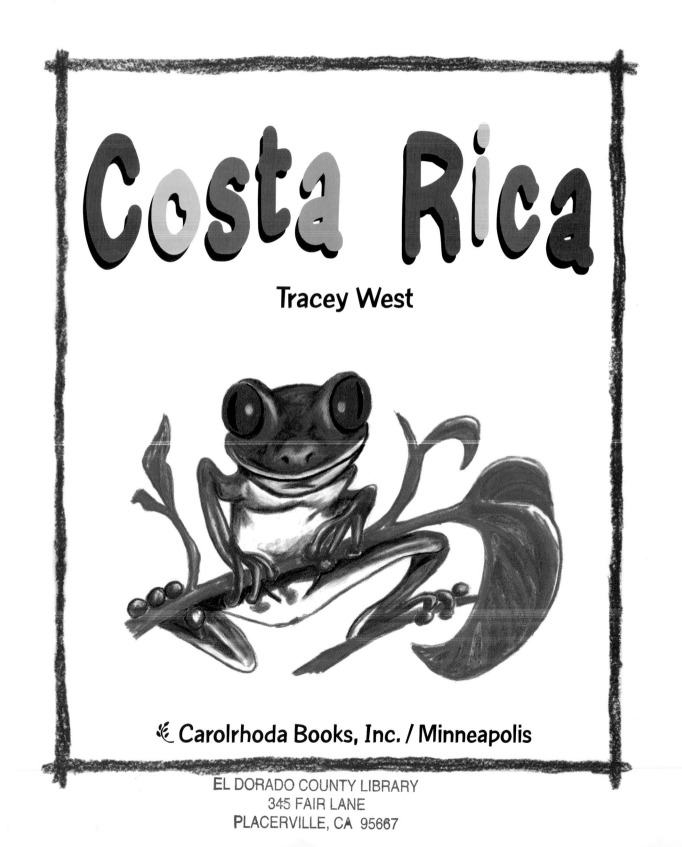

✿ Carolrhoda Books, Inc. / Minneapolis

Photo Acknowledgments

Photos, maps, and artwork are used courtesy of: John Erste, pp. 1, 2−3, 14−15, 22, 31, 33, 35; Laura Westlund pp. 4−5, 17; Martha Kranes, pp. 6 (left), 22, 30, 31 (right), 34; © Buddy Mays/Travel Stock, pp. 6 (right), 11 (right), 15 (top), 23 (left), 42 (both); © Tom Boyden, pp. 7 (left), 9 (top), 36, 37 (right); © TRIP/D. Maybury, pp. 7 (right), 9 (bottom); © TRIP/R. Powers, pp. 8−9; Knights of Columbus Headquarters Museum, p. 10; © Robert Fried, pp. 12 (both), 15 (bottom), 16−17, 18 (top), 19, 20, 26 (right); © Link/Visuals Unlimited, p. 13; © Franklin Viola, pp. 14, 29, 31 (left), 39 (both); © George Loun/Visuals Unlimited, p. 16; © Erwin C. "Bud" Nielsen/Images International, pp. 24, 32; © Frank Balthis, pp. 18 (bottom), 40, 41 (right), 43, 44; © Dave Bryant/D. Donne Bryant Stock Photo, pp. 21 (left), 23 (right), 25 (bottom); painting by Aquiles Bigot, courtesy of Muséo Historico Cultural Juan Santamaría, p. 21 (right); © Jay Ireland & Georgienne E. Bradley, pp. 25 (top), 26 (left), 35; Agence France Presse/Corbis-Bettmann, p. 27; © Inga Spence/Visuals Unlimited, pp. 28, 45; © Terry Wolkerstorfer, p. 33; © D. Donne Bryant/D. Donne Bryant Stock Photo, p. 37 (left); © Brian A. Vikander, p. 38; © Al Buchanan/D. Donne Bryant Stock Photo, p. 41 (left). Cover photo of Costa Rican kids © Cory Langley.

Carolrhoda Books, Inc.
A Division of the Lerner Publishing Group
241 First Avenue North
Minneapolis, Minnesota 55401 U.S.A.

Website address: www.lernerbooks.com

Library of Congress Cataloging-in-Publication Data

West, Tracey, 1965−
    Costa Rica / by Tracey West.
        p.   cm. — (A ticket to)
    Includes index.
    Summary: Briefly describes the people, geography, government, religion, language, customs, and lifestyles of Costa Rica.
    ISBN 1−57505−134−6 (lib. bdg. : alk. paper)
    1. Costa Rica—Juvenile literature. [1. Costa Rica.] I. Title. II. Series.
F1543.2.W47 1999
972.86-dc21   98−53917

Manufactured in the United States of America
1 2 3 4 5 6 − JR − 04 03 02 01 00 99

Contents

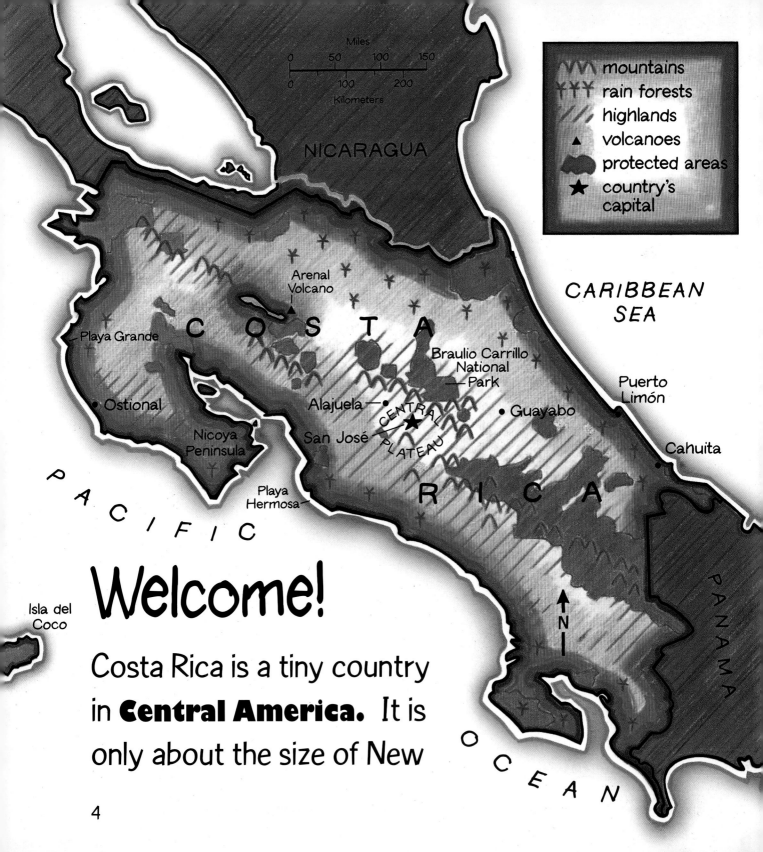

mountains
rain forests
highlands
▲ volcanoes
protected areas
★ country's capital

Miles
0   50   100   150
0   100   200
Kilometers

NICARAGUA

CARIBBEAN SEA

Arenal Volcano

C O S T A

Playa Grande

Braulio Carrillo National Park

Puerto Limón

Ostional

Alajuela

CENTRAL PLATEAU

Guayabo

San José

Cahuita

Nicoya Peninsula

R I C A

Playa Hermosa

P A C I F I C

N

Isla del Coco

Welcome!

Costa Rica is a tiny country in **Central America.** It is only about the size of New

PANAMA

O C E A N

4

Hampshire. Take a look at the **map.** Costa Rica snuggles between two countries. Nicaragua perches on the north, and Panama sits to the southeast. Costa Rica acts like a bridge between the two. Everywhere else there is water. The Caribbean Sea splashes the northeastern coast of Costa Rica, while the Pacific Ocean's waves roll up on the western and southwestern shores.

Map Whiz Quiz

Trace the map of Costa Rica on a piece of paper. Find Nicaragua and write an N for north. Put an S for south in the Pacific Ocean near Panama. See the Nicoya **Peninsula?** Mark that with a W for west. The Caribbean Sea gets an E for east. Now shade in the protected areas with a green crayon.

The wonders of the rain forest, such as bats, tree frogs, and three-toed sloths (above), *lie across this bridge* (left).

La Selva

Squish! Squish! Squish! That is the sound of a hiker walking a muddy trail in *la selva* (the jungle). Jungles, or **tropical rain forests,** get rain almost every day.

Leaf-cutter ants carry rain-forest leaves to their underground garden.

Costa Rica is near the **equator,** so it has warm temperatures all year round. Rain and heat make a steamy combination— perfect for lots of plants and animals.

Beautiful Birds

Fascinating plants and animals live in Costa Rica's rain forests. Toucans, parrots, and a rare bird called the quetzal *(left)* all live there. Many people think the quetzal is one of the most beautiful birds in the world!

Up High

Rain forests line the country's low, flat coasts. **Mountains** bulge up in the middle and ring the Central Valley. In the middle of the valley lies the Central **Plateau.**

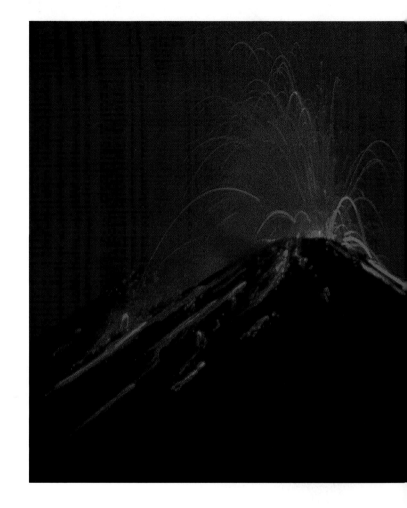

Of Costa Rica's mountains, more than 100 are **volcanoes.** But only 7 still erupt. Over hundreds of years, volcanic **lava** and ash have turned the Central Valley into rich farmland.

Sandy Shores

When lava cools, it becomes hard, black rock. Thousands of years ago, lava oozed its way to Costa Rica's coast. Pounding ocean waves smashed the lava until it turned to sand. That is why some parts of Costa Rica's coastline have black beaches!

Arenal Volcano (above) shoots hot, melted rock called lava into the sky. Coffee plants (inset) grow well in the Central Valley's rich volcanic soil.

Land, Ho!

Long ago Christopher Columbus and his crew first set eyes on Costa Rica. The *indígenas* (native peoples) who lived there greeted the newcomers. The indígenas wore

Christopher Columbus and his crew stepped onto Costa Rica's shores in 1502. But the indígenas had already been living there for thousands of years.

beautiful costumes and gold jewelry. The Spanish explorers hoped to find lots of gold. They called the area Costa Rica, which means "rich coast" in the Spanish language. Although not much gold was found, settlers came from Spain to farm the rich soil. Most Costa Ricans can trace their **ancestors** to Spanish settlers and to indígenas. People of mixed Spanish and indígena backgrounds are called mestizos.

An indígena family paddles along in a dugout canoe. Many indígenas carry on the traditional ways of their ancestors.

First People

A young indígena boy learns to weave a basket from his father (above). An indígena dwelling (top) is made of local plant materials.

The indígenas lived in Costa Rica long before Columbus landed there. They hunted and farmed for food. They made cloth, baskets, pottery, and jewelry by hand. They built whole cities and

A Mystery

Long, long ago, an indígena group lived near the present-day town of Guayabo. But 600 years ago, the townspeople mysteriously disappeared. These days the ancient town is deserted, but traces of the village still exist. Stone roads wind along the earth, and pillars rise from the ground. They are decorated with carved designs of jaguars and alligators. No one knows for sure who built this town—or why it was abandoned.

decorated them with stone carvings. Only about 10,000 indígenas still live in Costa Rica. Most live in small communities on land set aside by the government.

In an indígena community, pottery is still made the old-fashioned way—by hand.

Before it was shut down in 1990, the Jungle Train carried passengers through miles of thick, wet rain forest.

Jungle Train

A railroad once linked the cities of San José and Puerto Limón. Thousands of people came from other countries to help lay tracks for the Jungle Train. Those workers from Britain, Jamaica, Italy, and China have added to the mix of Costa Ricans. Since then more people have come to Costa Rica.

Newcomers to Costa Rica include Nicaraguans, or *nicas. Many come to find jobs on the country's coffee and banana farms.*

Ticos

Costa Ricans have nicknamed themselves *ticos.* The ancestors of the people living in Costa Rica may have come from all over. But no matter what their background is, they are proud to be called ticos.

This tico has Jamaican ancestors.

Josefinos can find fresh produce at one of San José's many outdoor markets.

City Life

Buildings crowd San José's sidewalks. Traffic never seems to stop. *Josefinos* (ticos who live in San José) like the fast-paced city life.

Most josefinos live in row houses—look-alike homes that are attached to one another. Others live in larger houses just outside the city. Very poor residents

16

Dear Grandpa,

San José is fun! Yesterday we spent the morning in la **Plaza** de la Cultura. People set up shop and sell all kinds of crafts. Mom let me pick out a bamboo flute. We sat and watched a magician do tricks, and the group of indígena musicians played great music. After lunch we stopped at the Gold Museum. Everything we saw was made thousands of years ago! Tomorrow we are going on a hike through a rain forest. See you soon!

Love,
Abigail

Sun Mainitian
Waum Kaillian
Thalurihu, Simla
730N, Laurathin

live in dwellings of wood and metal. Many different people call San José home.

Mountains make for a grand view from downtown San José.

Life in the countryside (left) *can be quiet and relaxing. Out of toothpaste? Need some soap? Better make a trip to la pulpería* (below).

Campesinos

Some *campesinos* (country dwellers) live in large, colorful houses. Others build small cottages of adobe, a kind of brick. For events, campesinos gather in the plaza, usually located in the center of town. Another fun place to hang out is *la pulpería—*

a general store that sells everything from hardware to candy. Campesinos often grow their own food and sell the extra goods at local markets. Everyone helps out on the family farm.

All in the Family

Here are the Spanish names for family members.

grandfather	*abuelo*	(ah-BWAY-loh)
grandmother	*abuela*	(ah-BWAY-lah)
father	*padre*	(PAH-dray)
mother	*madre*	(MAH-dray)
uncle	*tío*	(TEE-oh)
aunt	*tía*	(TEE-ah)
son	*hijo*	(EE-hoh)
daughter	*hija*	(EE-hah)
brother	*hermano*	(ehr-MAH-noh)
sister	*hermana*	(ehr-MAH-nah)

School Days

Get out your books! Costa Rican kids between the ages of 7 and 14 go to school. Getting dressed in the morning is a snap. Everybody wears a uniform to school. Kids dress in blue or white shirts and blue pants or skirts.

City kids go to class in a big school building. But students in the country may attend small one-room schoolhouses.

Kids on a school trip to Poas Volcano National Park learn about the wonders of their country.

A Vote for Education

Education is very important in Costa Rica. In fact, Costa Rica's former president José María Castro Madriz was once a teacher himself!

Students study reading, math, and social studies. Classes learn about taking care of the environment, too. Kids learn about protecting the rain forest in their own neighborhoods!

A campesina makes bread the traditional way, in an outdoor oven. The loaves are baked on banana leaves!

Food

Rise and shine!

Time for some *gallo pinto*—that means "spotted rooster." Gallo pinto (beans and rice) is eaten for breakfast. If you use your imagination, you can see the speckled bird on your plate. At lunch or dinner, ticos eat tortillas stuffed with beef, chicken, beans, or

Many fast-food restaurants from the United States have found their way to Costa Rica.

pork. A special treat is *la olla*—a soup made of beef and vegetables.

Seafood stew is a hit among ticos.

Bananas, mangoes, papayas, and pineapples make tasty desserts. Many ticos can pick tropical fruits straight from trees in their own backyards!

La Playa

La playa (the beach) in Costa Rica is never far away. Ticos who want to check out sea turtles can head to la Playa Grande. Surfers prefer la Playa Hermosa. The clear, Caribbean waters near Cahuita let scuba divers get an up-close look at beautiful coral reefs. Costa Rica has plenty of other fun things to do.

Temperatures on the coasts (facing page) *hover in the 80s all year— perfect beach weather! A bike ride with friends* (left) *can be great fun and good exercise.*

Kids like to play soccer, go to the movies, or watch TV. Ticos might make special trips to San José to see a play.

Theater lovers enjoy going to plays at el Teatro Nacional (the National Theater) in San José.

Ranchers raise cattle in northwestern Costa Rica, often called the "Texas of Costa Rica."

Play Time!

Kids practice their soccer moves.

Fútbol means "soccer" in Spanish. Kids play soccer whenever and wherever they can. Any open spot can become a soccer field. Professionals play at el Estadio

A Costa Rican soccer player (in red and blue) tries to get a pass by his Jamaican defender.

Nacional (the National Stadium) in San José. Folks who prefer a different kind of excitement will find it in northwestern Costa Rica, an area famous for its **rodeo** contests. Cowboys ride on the backs of bulls, while the angry beasts buck and kick. Hang on tight!

Religion

Nine out of ten Costa Ricans follow the Roman Catholic faith (the religion of Spain). Other folks are Protestants. Many Protestants have Jamaican ancestors and live on the Caribbean coast. Some indígenas practice their traditional religions.

A Roman Catholic basilica (church) near San José

Ticos celebrate Good Friday (the Friday before Easter) with a parade through the center of town.

Ticos celebrate Easter with a bang! The fireworks begin when the sun rises on Easter morning and keep popping all day and night. People watch parades, bullfights, rodeos, and dances.

Proud to Be Tico

Ticos are proud of their country and its history. They celebrate special days with parades and parties. El Día de la Raza (Columbus Day) is the biggest holiday. Celebrations last for four days, as ticos remember the long-ago day when Christopher Columbus arrived in their land.

Dressed as the first Spanish settlers, young ticos ride a float during a parade to celebrate el Día de la Raza.

Towns in Costa Rica have yearly celebrations to show community spirit. Children take turns batting a piñata—a papier-mâché figure filled with candy.

A statue in Alajuela represents Juan Santamaría. As a young boy, Juan helped the Costa Rican army win a major battle in 1865.

Thumbs Up!

Costa Ricans take election days seriously. Everyone comes out to vote and to celebrate. People dip their thumbs in purple ink to show that they voted. There are many purple thumbs in sight on election day. That is because 8 out of 10 people vote!

What Army?

Costa Rica is a peaceful country. To keep the peace, Costa Rica has a national guard instead of an army. Guardsmen and women patrol the streets during national events.

Members of the national guard march in a parade honoring one of Costa Rica's national holidays.

Boy Scouts

When the president of Costa Rica gives a speech to a large crowd, who does he call? The Boy Scouts! They often stand up with the president when he appears in public.

Tico scouts share their knowledge with Boy Scouts from the United States.

Costa Rica spends money on health care and education, not on military equipment.

Red, white, and blue are the colors in Costa Rica's flag.

Listen Up!

Tico music blends the sounds of the indígenas, the Caribbean peoples, and

Indígena musicians perform in San José.

the Spaniards. Sway to the tunes of indígena instruments such as the *chirimía* (similar to an oboe) and the *quijongo* (a single-stringed instrument with a hollow bowl that vibrates). The funky beat of tico folk music is played on the marimba (a huge xylophone made

Boogey Down!

City people groove to popular music in discos. But some like to strut their stuff on the dance floor with traditional moves. Folk dances include the cumbia, the merengue, the salsa, and the lambada.

with wooden bars). This instrument originally came from Africa. When musicians strike a bar with a mallet, a hollow bowl vibrates. Guitar players often strum along with the marimba music.

Oldest Art

Many people have used the stone spheres to decorate their lawns.

What is perfectly round and made out of
stone? One of Costa Rica's greatest mysteries.
Ancient peoples had carved stone spheres
(balls). Some weigh as much as 16 tons and
measure 8 feet across! No one knows how or
why these spheres were made. One can be

Art Carts

The painted *carreta* (oxcart) is one of Costa Rica's famous art forms. Oxcarts were used to transport coffee beans over mountain roads. The carreta had special wheels to help the driver cut through sticky mud. Trucks and trains have replaced the oxcart, but artists still paint the colorful wagons.

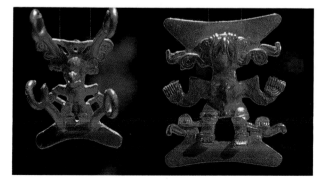

El Museo del Oro (the Gold Museum) in San José holds hundreds of gold objects made by Costa Rica's early peoples.

seen in the National Museum in San José. The National Museum has some of the oldest art in Costa Rica.

Part of the movie Jurassic Park *was filmed in Braulio Carrillo National Park.*

Explore the Land

Costa Rica has more than 30 national parks. Visitors to these protected areas can learn about growing plants, rumbling volcanoes, or flying insects. People visiting Braulio Carrillo National Park can ride the Rain-Forest Aerial

The coast of la Isla del Coco

Tram. Another national park, la Isla del Coco (Coconut Island), is covered with jungles, waterfalls, and coconut trees.

Sharks!

Visitors come to la Isla del Coco to see the island's great beauty. Scuba divers get a close-up look at underwater caves and coral gardens. Not to mention sharks!

Hammerhead sharks and white-tipped sharks swim near the island. Swimmers may see hundreds of sharks at once!

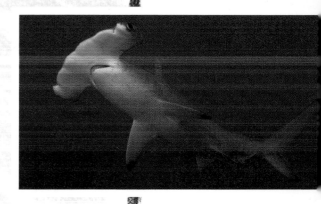

In September and October, sea turtles lay their eggs on Costa Rica's beaches. Each female lays up to 100 eggs in the sand.

Turtle Tales

Every year hundreds of female sea turtles crawl up the beach near the village of Ostional. They lay their eggs in the warm sand. When the eggs hatch, thousands of baby turtles flop to the sea. But not all of the eggs survive. Animals dig up many before they hatch.

The villagers of Ostional protect the nests. When the eggs hatch, the villagers make sure the baby turtles get to sea without being eaten by animals.

A sea snake (below) is one type of animal that eats sea-turtle eggs.

Scientists weigh sea turtles (above) to collect information.

National parks help protect Costa Rica's treasured rain forests (left). A lot of rain-forest land is cleared for farmland and pasture (above).

Save the Trees!

Farmers and ranchers clear rain forests for farmland and grazing land. Companies cut trees to make paper and building materials. But trees help keep the world's air clean. Some Costa Ricans want to protect their rain forests and to stop rain-forest destruction. The government sets aside land as parks and protected areas. Kids learn about protecting the rain forest in school. Ecotourism is another way of saving Costa Rica's rain forests. It works like this. Tourists from around the world visit Costa Rica's parks. Ticos make money from the tourists year after year without having to cut down trees.

Ecotourists enjoy a natural hot spring on the slopes of one of Costa Rica's volcanoes.

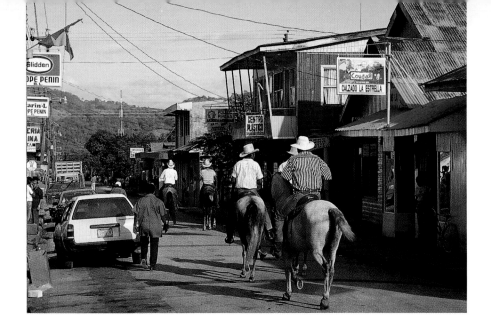

Many campesinos still use horses to get around town.

New Words to Learn

ancestor: A long-ago relative, such as a great-great-great grandparent.

Central America: The narrow southern portion of North America that connects that continent to South America. The countries of Central America are Guatemala, El Salvador, Honduras, Nicaragua, Costa Rica, Panama, and Belize.

equator: An imaginary line that circles the globe at the middle, dividing the world into a northern half and a southern half.

lava: Hot, liquid rock that comes out of an erupting volcano.

map: A drawing or chart of all or part of the earth or sky.

mountain: Part of the earth's surface that rises into the sky.

peninsula: A piece of land that has water on three of its sides. The fourth side is connected to land.

plateau: A large area of high, level land.

plaza: A public square, usually centrally located in a town.

rodeo: A contest usually performed on horseback. Rodeo events include roping calves and riding bulls.

tropical rain forest: A thick, green forest that gets lots of rain every year.

volcano: An opening in the earth's surface through which hot, melted rock shoots up. Volcano can also mean the hill or mountain of ash and rock that builds up around the opening.

Oxcarts haul goods.

New Words to Say

Cahuita	cah-WEE-tah
campesinos	cahm-pay-SEE-nohs
chirimía	chee-ree-MEE-ah
Costa Rica	COHS-tah REE-kah
Estadio Nacional	ay-STAH-dee-oh nah-see-oh-NAHL
fútbol	FOOT-bohl
gallo pinto	GAH-yoh PEEN-toh
indígenas	een-DEE-hay-nahs
josefinos	hoh-say-FEE-nohs
Juan Santamaría	WAHN sahn-tah-mah-REE-ah
la olla	lah OH-yah
la playa	lah PLY-ah
mestizos	mays-TEE-sohs
Ostional	ohs-tee-oh-NAL
Plaza de la Cultura	PLA-sah day lah cool-TOO-rah
Puerto Limón	PWEHR-toh lee-MOHN
pulpería	pool-pay-REE-ah
quetzal	kayt-SAHL
quijongo	kee-HOHN-goh
San José	SAHN hoh-SAY

46

More Books to Read

Baden, Robert. *And Sunday Makes Seven.* Niles, IL: A. Whitman, 1990.

Baskin-Salzberg, Anita and Allen Salzberg. *Turtles.* New York: Franklin Watts, 1996.

Berman, Ruth. *Climbing Tree Frogs.* Minneapolis: Lerner Publications Company, 1998.

Foran, Eileen. *Costa Rica is My Home.* Milwaukee: Gareth Stevens, 1992.

Lewington, Anna. *Antonio's Rain Forest.* Minneapolis: Carolrhoda Books, Inc., 1993.

Oldfield, Sara. *Rain Forests.* Minneapolis: Lerner Publications Company, 1996.

Patent, Dorothy Hinshaw. *Children Save the Rain Forest.* New York: Cobblehill Books, 1996.

Sauvain, Philip. *Rain Forests.* Minneapolis: Carolrhoda Books, Inc., 1997.

Sousa, D.M. *Frogs, Frogs Everywhere.* Minneapolis: Carolrhoda Books, Inc., 1994.

Temko, Florence. *Traditional Crafts from Mexico and Central America.* Minneapolis: Lerner Publications Company, 1996.

New Words to Find